21 TARA
Paintings

SUSANNE ISABEL KRAJANEK

ISBN-10: 154108750X

ISBN-13: 978-1541087507

DEDICATION

Dedicated to all the Pilgrims travelling between the high mountains and the endless plains of northern India.

Dedicated to Gangotri at the source of the River Ganga and to Bodhgaya in Bihar.

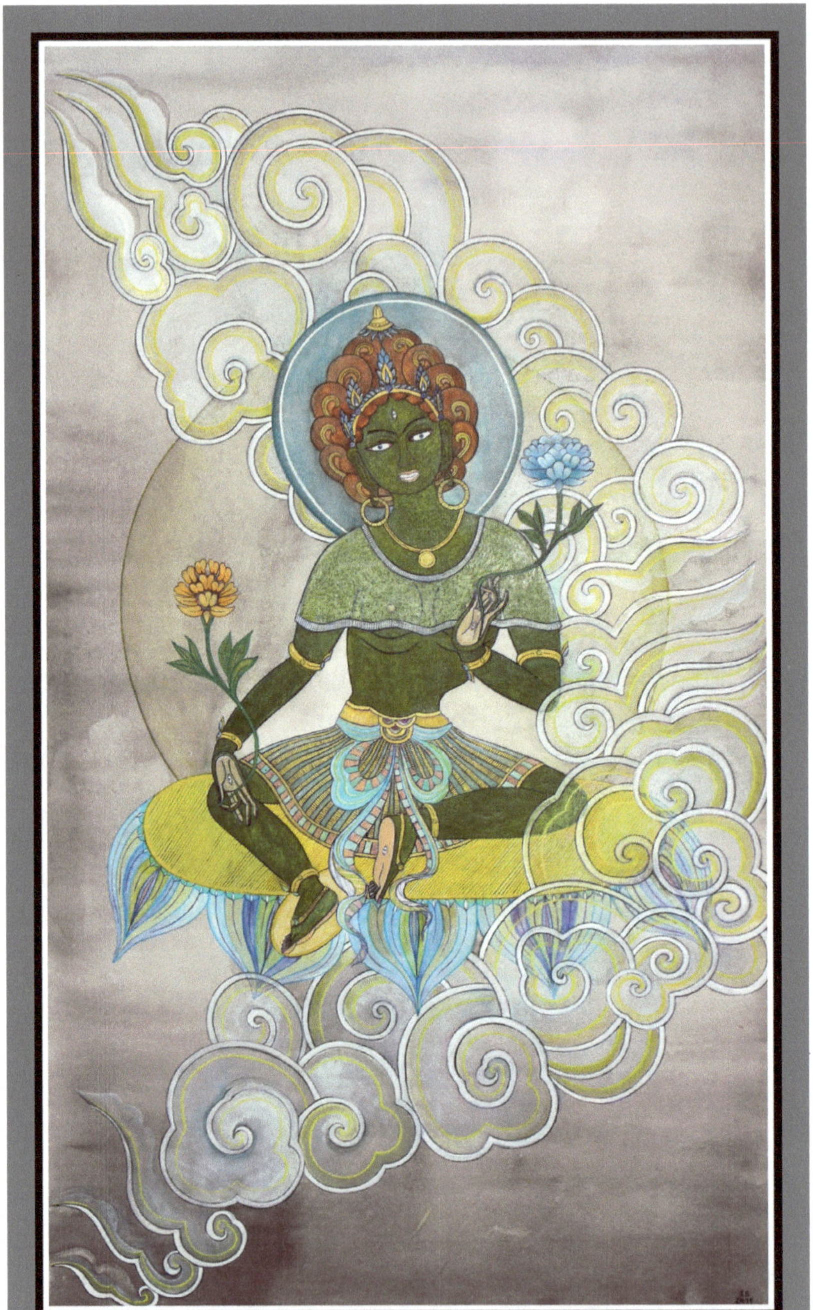

CONTENTS

8 Tārā Who Crushes All Maras and Bestows Supreme Powers

Māra-sūdanā vasittôtama-da-tārā

9 Tārā Granter of Boons

Vara-da-tārā

10 Tārā Dispelling All Sorrow

Śoka-vinodana-tārā

11 Tārā Summoner of All Beings, Dispeller of All Misfortune,

Jagad-vaśī vipan-nirbarhaṇa-tārā

12 Tārā Giver of All Prosperity

Kalyāna-da-tārā

13 Tārā the Ripener

Paripācaka-tārā

14 Tārā the Wrathful Summoner

Bhṛkuṭī-tārā

15 Tārā the Great Peaceful One

Māha-śānti-tārā

16 Tārā Destroyer of All Attachement

Rāga-niṣūdana-tārā

PREFACE

I painted these pictures of the 21 forms of Tara between 1990 and 2014, mostly in Bodhgaya and in the Upper Ganga valley in India.

The explanations and description of the Iconographies I found at first in Martin Willsons book 'In Praise of Tara' and also in the encyclopedia of Buddhist icons 'Deities of Tibetan Buddhism-The Zurich Paintings of the Icons Worthwhile to See' by Martin Willson, Martin Brauen and Robert Beer.

I was very happy to see the small block-prints and learn about these iconographic descriptions how to depict the Goddess Tara's twenty-one forms, which originated in India and is very different from later, more widely known, iconographies.

As I spend a good part of my life in India I wanted to paint according to those scriptures and over long years these colorful goddesses were my companions, teaching me in the art of painting.

I started to paint Taras in 1991 in Bodhgaya with the thirteenth form, who is called 'Tara the Ripener' and finished the first complete series of twenty-one some years later in 1996 with the eighteenth, 'Tara the Victorious'. I did not follow the order, but worked according to my situation.

In the following years I gave many of my Tara paintings away privately and during exhibitions in India and Austria. But the whole time I tried to keep the series of all twenty-one complete and painted some in different versions again and again, changing backgrounds and ornaments, but always kept close to the given original iconography, like body color, hand signs and attributes.

Finally, in 2016, as my very first picture, 'Tara, the Ripener' was taken home by a little girl, I completed the circle of so many paintings, with a new version of 'Tara, the Ripener'.

In this book I want to show the actual series of paintings, as I have them now. They are really quite small, only 20 cm x 20 cm, worked painstakingly fine with brush only, watercolor on paper.

I added to each painting the original Sanskrit name and verse , as I found them in Martin Willson's book and also an English translation.

All further explanations about the Buddhist Goddess Tara, if sought for, can be found in the scholars' books, because I wanted to paint only.

1 . TĀRĀ SWIFT AND HEROIC
PRAVĪRA-TĀRĀ

namas tāre ture vīre
kṣaṇair-dyuti-nibhêkhṣaṇe
trailokya-nātha-vaktrâbja
vikasat-keśarôdbhave

Homage! Tārā, swift heroine,
Every look like flash of lightening!
Sprung from tears like op'ning stamens
from Lord of Three Worlds' facial lotus.

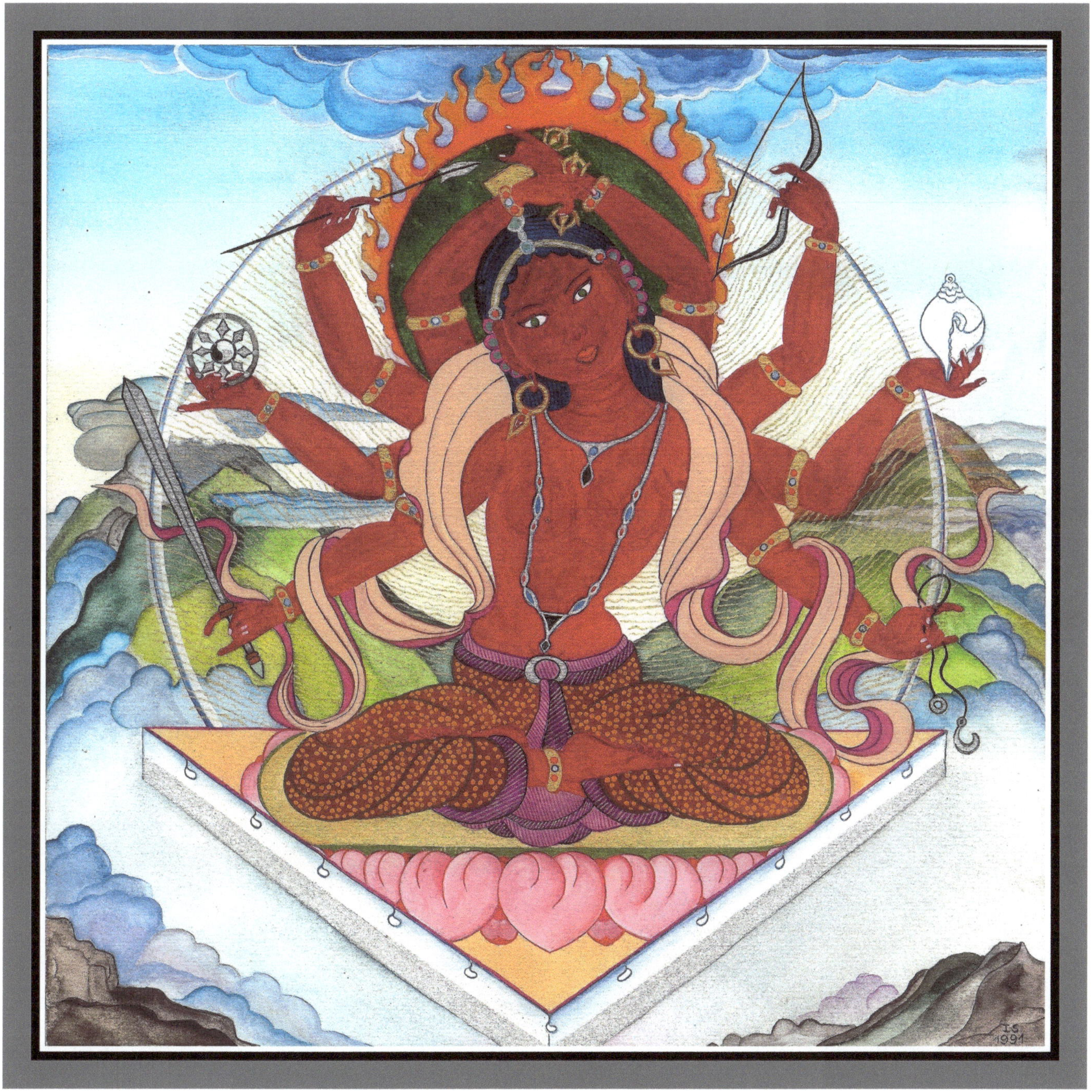
I.S.
1991

2 . TĀRĀ, WHITE AS THE AUTUMN MOON
CANDRA-KĀNTI-TĀRĀ

namaḥ śata-śarac-candra-
saṃpūrṇa-paṭalânae
tārā-sahasra-nikara
prahasat-kiraṇôjjvale

Homage! Her, Whose face is shining
Like a hundred moons in autumn!
Emanating blazing light-rays
Like a thousand stars combined.

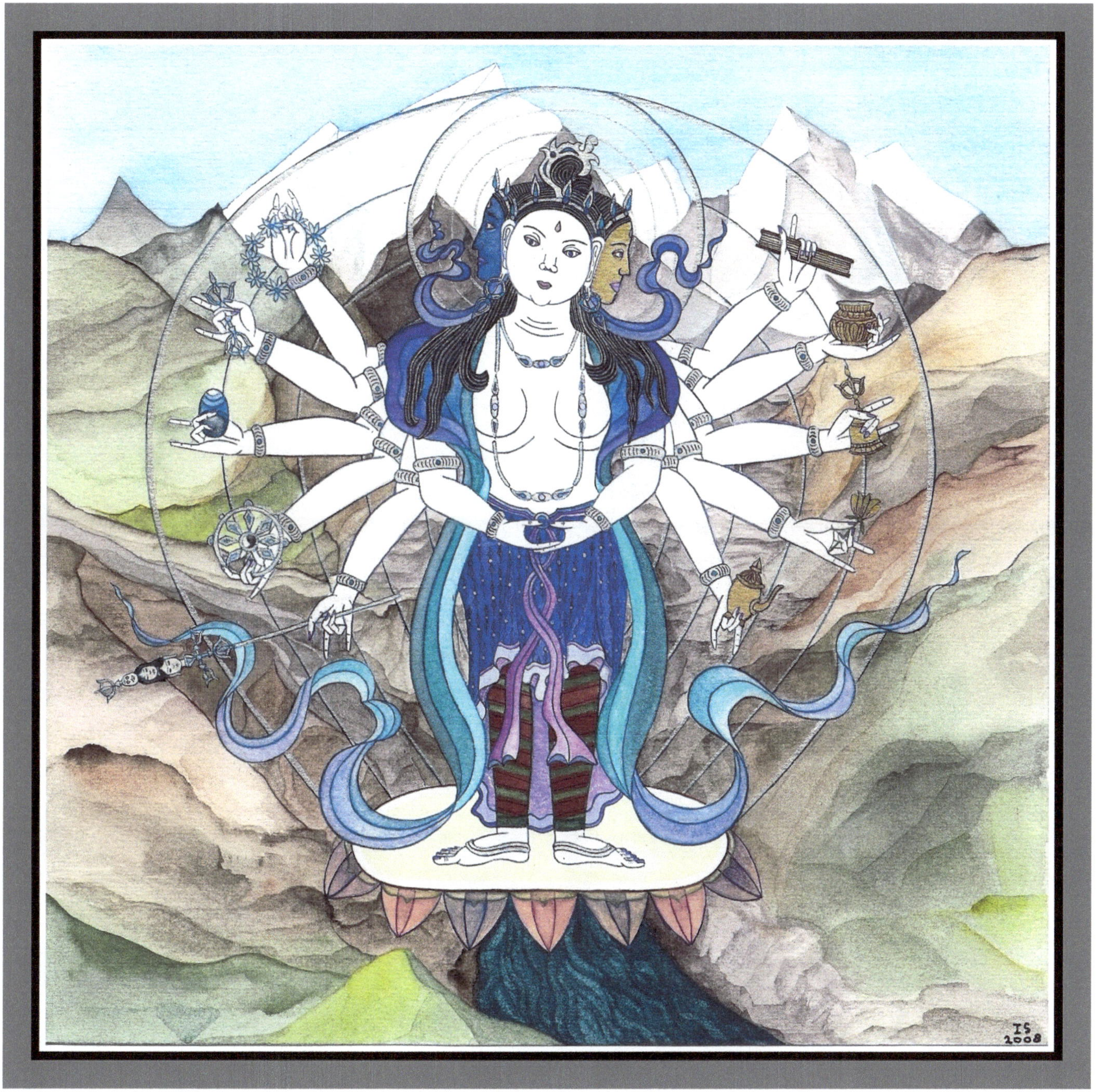
IS
2008

3 . TĀRĀ OF THE PERFECTIONS
KANAKA-VAṚNA-TĀRĀ

namaḥ kanaka-nīlâbja-
pāṇi-padma-vibhūṣite
dāna-vīrya-tapaḥ-śānti-
titikṣā-dhyāna-gocare

Homage! Golden One, water-born,
Hands adorn blue lotus flowers!
Her field calm, renunciation,
effort, patience, meditation.

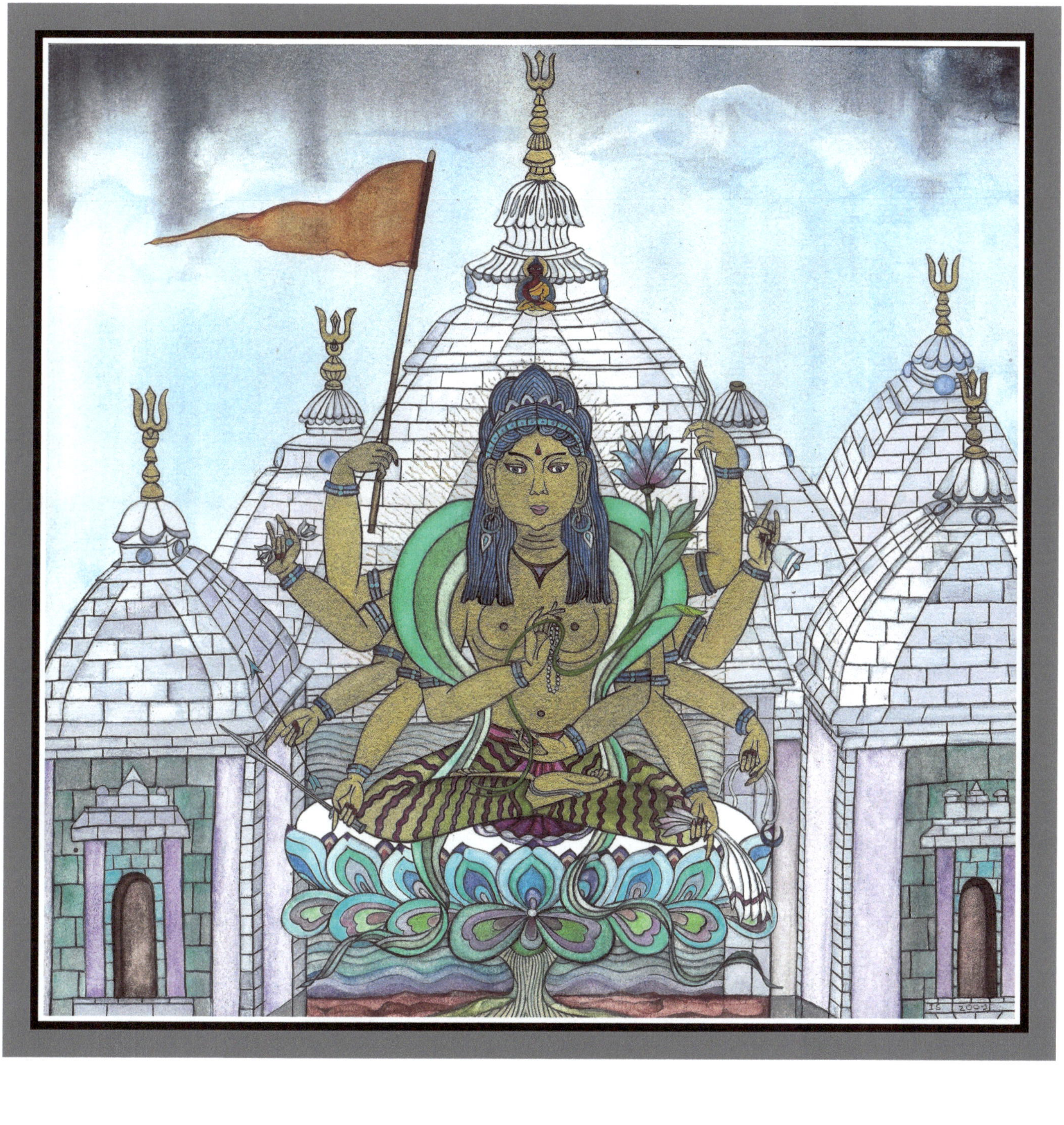
IS 2001

4. TĀRĀ, THE VICTORIOUS UṢṆIṢA OF TATHĀGATAS
UṢṆIṢA-VIJAYA-TĀRĀ

namas tathāgatôṣnīṣa-
vijayânanta-cāriṇi
aśeṣa-pāramitā-prāpta-
jina-putra-niṣevite

Homage! Crown of *Tathāgatas*,
Who goes on in endless triumph!
Honored by conqueror's children,
Mother reaching All Perfections.

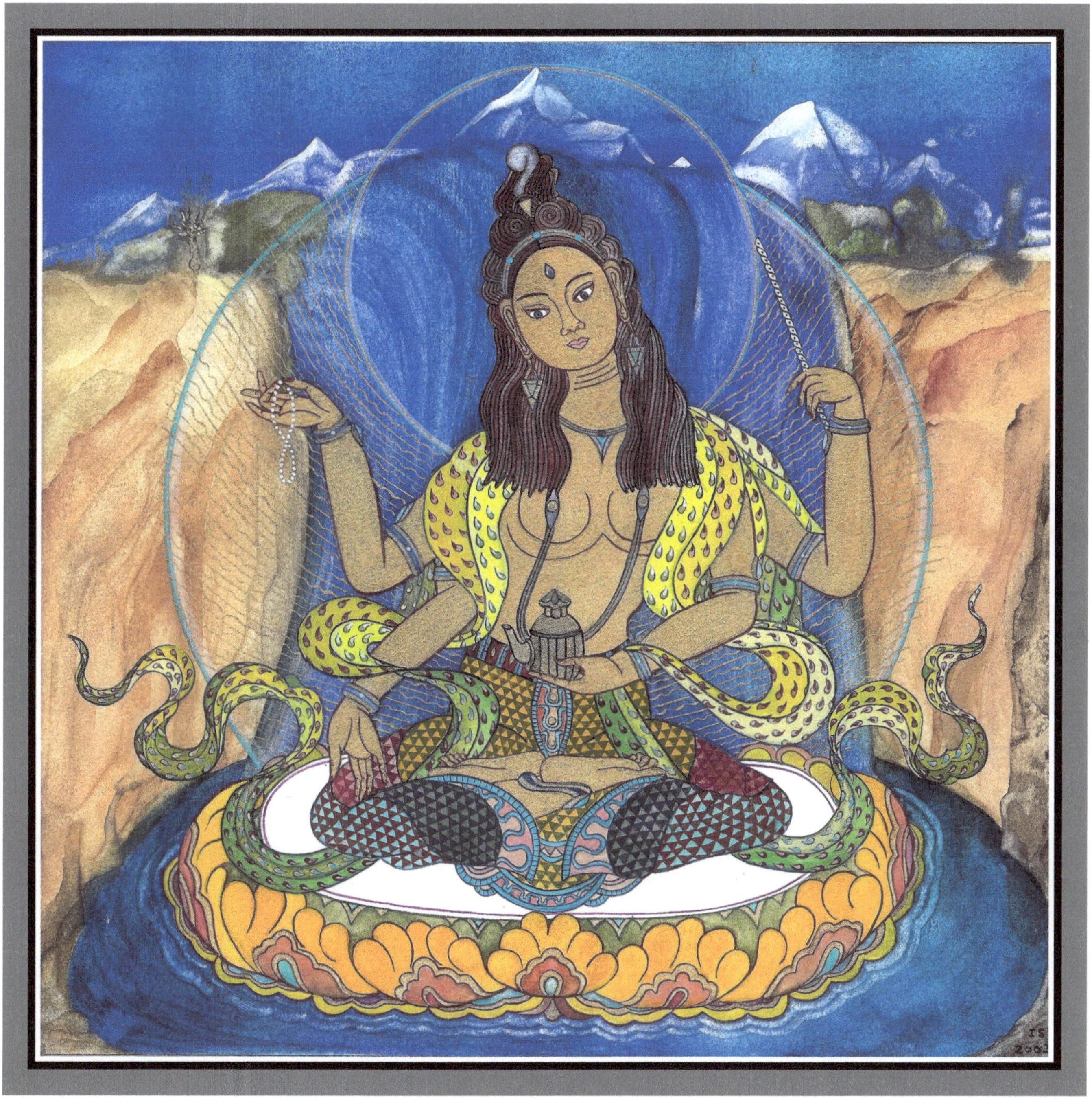

5. TĀRĀ PROCLAIMING THE SOUND OF HŪṂ
HŪṂ-SVARA-NĀDINĪ-TĀRĀ

namas tuttāra-hūm-kāra-
puritâśā-dig-antare
sapta-loka-kramâkrānti
aśeṣâkarṣaṇa-kṣame

Homage! Her, with TUTTARA HUM
Filling regions and space-quarters!
Trampling Seven Worlds with Her feet,
Taking control of all beings.

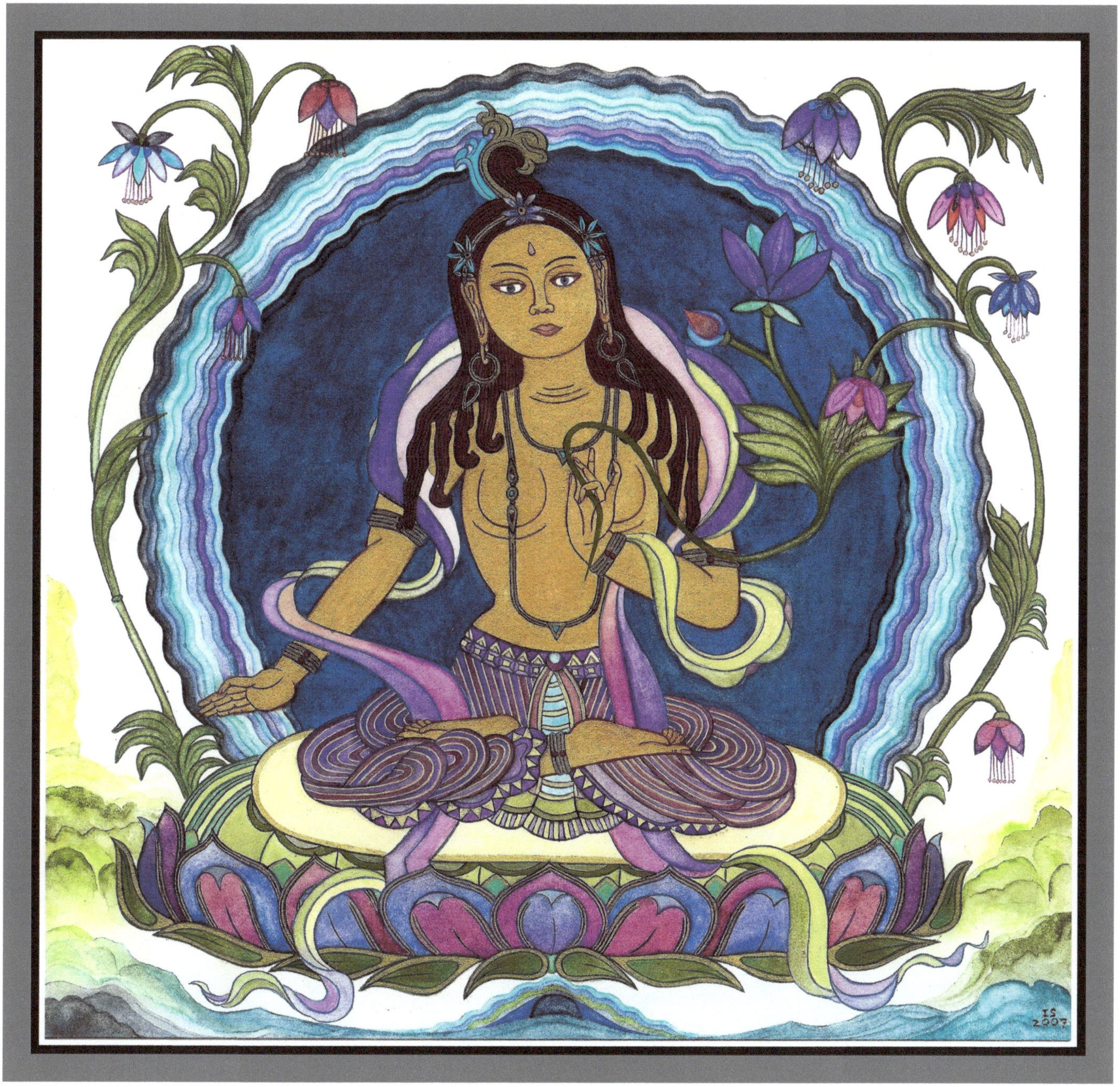
IS
2007

6. TĀRĀ VICTORIOUS OVER THE THREE WORLDS
TRAILOKYA-VIJAYA-TĀRĀ

namaḥ śakrânala-brahma-
marud-viśvêśvarârcite
bhūta-vetāla-gandharva-
gaṇa-yakṣa-puras-kṛte

Homage! Worshipped by the Great Lords,
Śakra, Agni, Brahmā, Marut!
Honored too by hosts of spirits
All *Bhūtas, Yakṣhas, Gandharvas.*

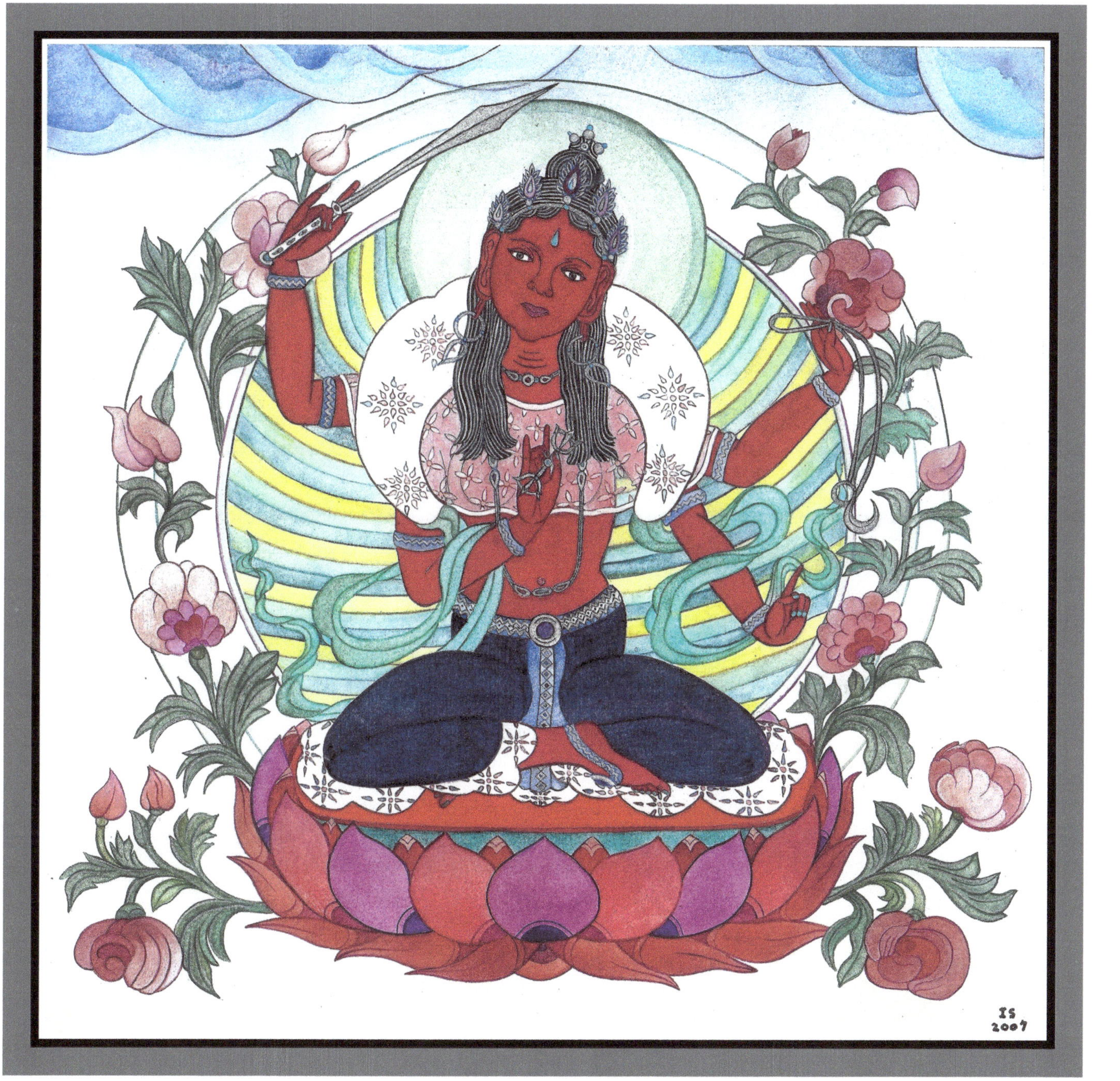
IS
2007

7. TĀRĀ CRUSHING ADVERSARIES
VĀDI-PRAMARDAKA-TĀRĀ

namas traḍ iti phat-kāra-
para-yantra-pramardani
praty-ālīḍha-pada-nyāse
śikhi-jvālakulêkṣaṇe

Homage! Her shouting TRAT and PHAT,
Crushing all en'mies dreadful snares!
With left foot outstretched, right foot back,
eyes alight with blazing fire.

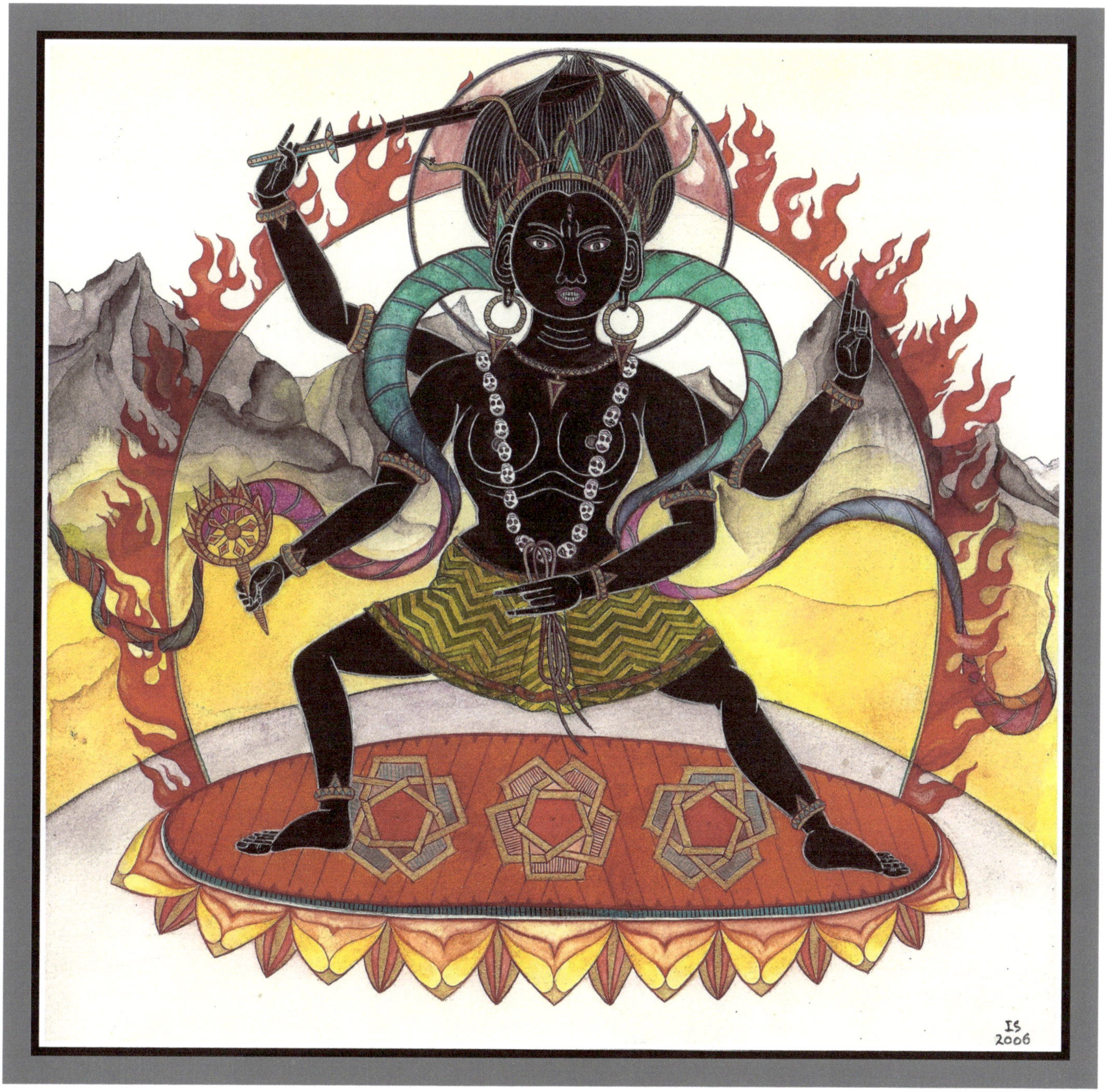
IS
2006

8. TĀRĀ WHO CRUSHES ALL MARAS AND BESTOWS SUPREME POWERS
MĀRA-SŪDANĀ VASITTÔTAMA-DA-TĀRĀ

namas ture mahā-ghore
māra-vīra-vināśani
bhṛkuṭī-kṛta-vaktrâbja-
sarva-śatru-niṣūdani

Homage! TURE, very wrathful,
Slaying *Mara's* forces all!
Lotus-face so very frowning,
it will destroy all enemies.

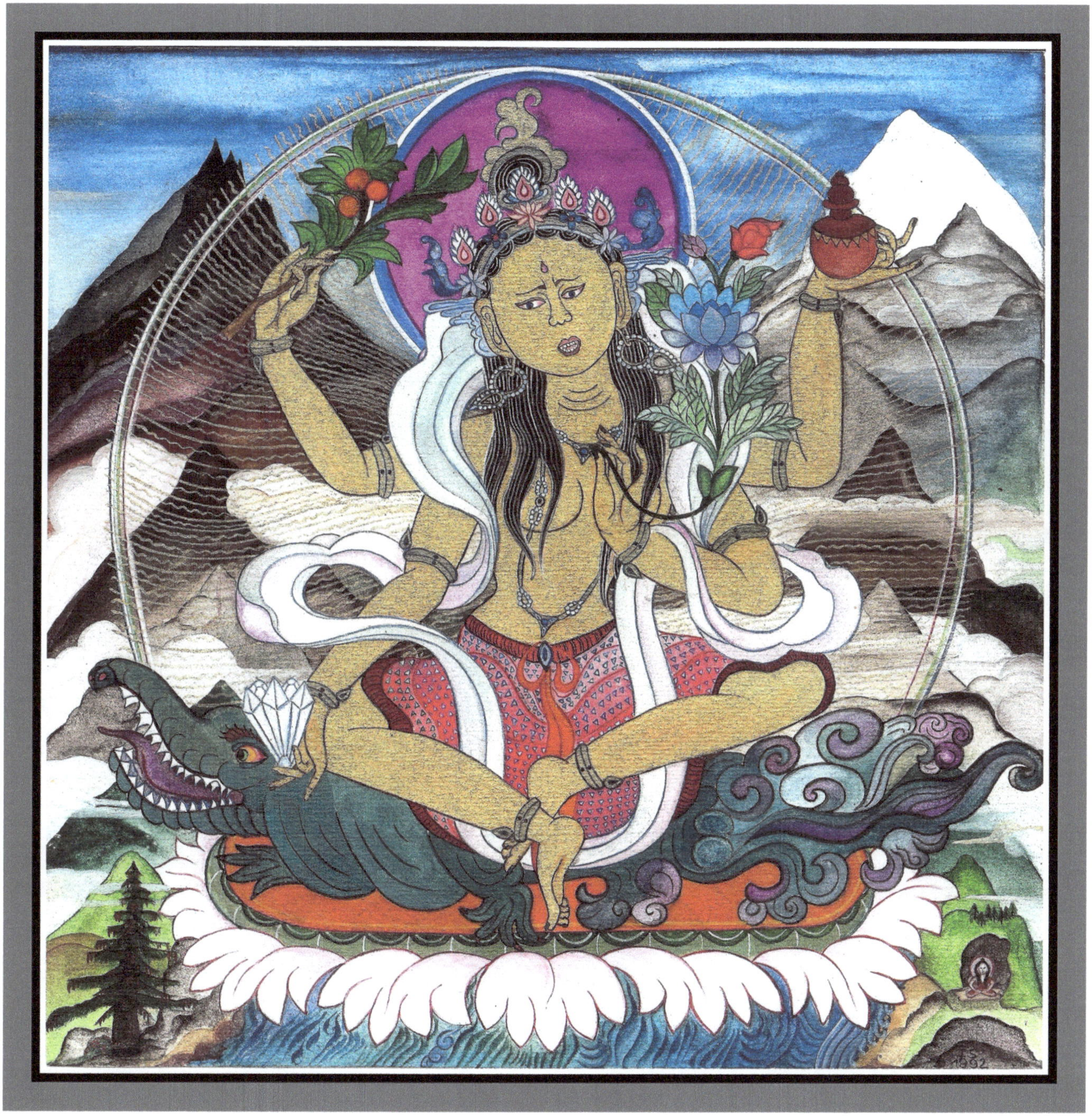
1992

9. TĀRĀ GRANTER OF BOONS
VARA-DA-TĀRĀ

namas tri-ratna-mudrâṅka-
hṛdyânguli-vibhūṣite
bhuṣitâśeṣa-dik-cakra-
nikara-sva-karâkule

Homage! Her, Whose fingers form
Three Jewel's *Mudra* at Her heart!
All Direction's Wheel adorns Her,
All quarters fill with Her own light.

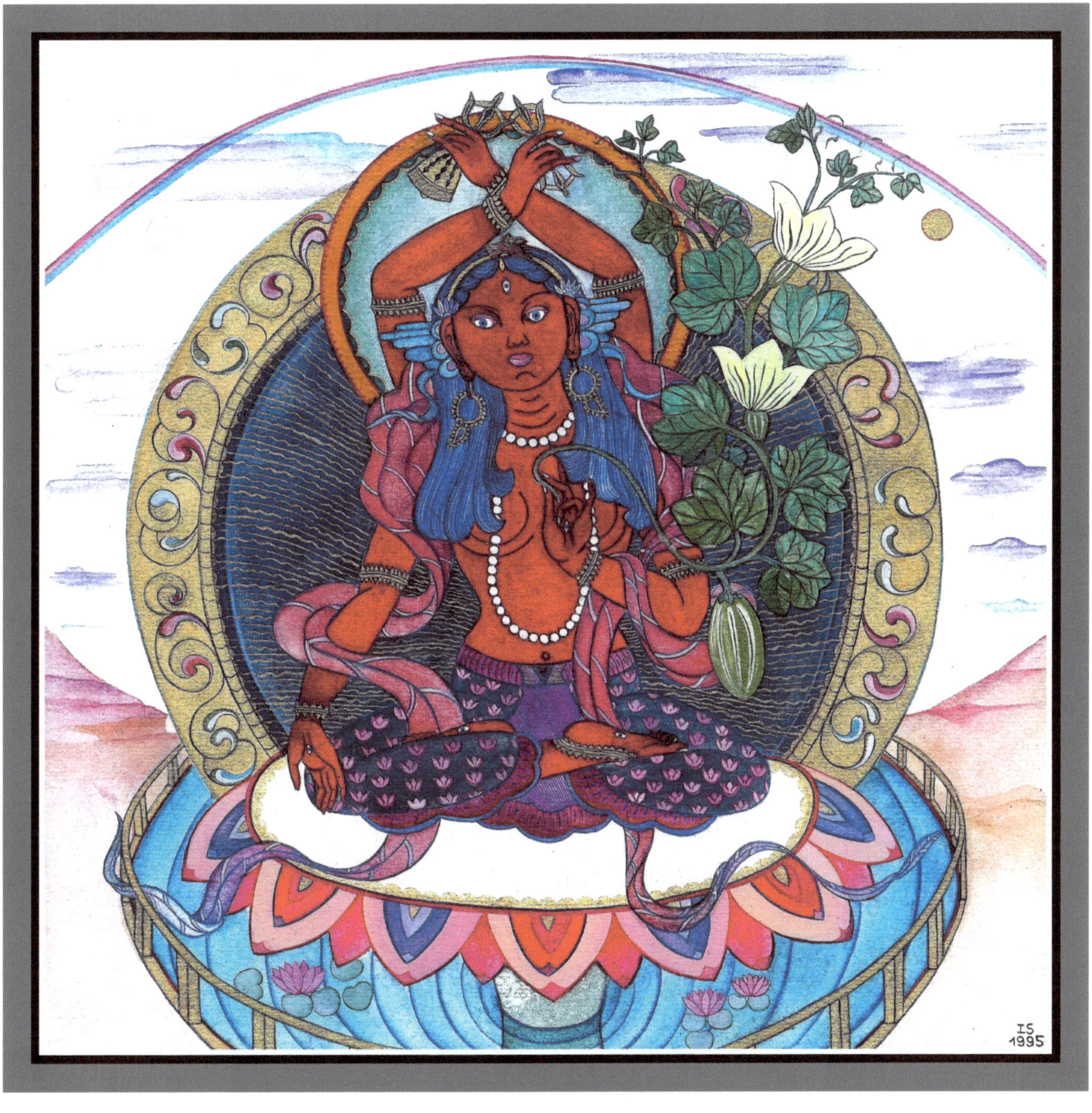
IS
1995

10. TĀRĀ DISPELLING ALL SORROW
ŚOKA-VINODANA-TĀRĀ

namaḥ pramuditâṭopa-
mukuṭā-kṣipta-mālini
hasat-prahasat-tuttāre
māra-loka-vaśaṃkari

Homage! Filled with swelling great joy,
Light garlands emitting diadem!
Mirthful laughter of TUTTARE
Subjugating *Devas, Maras.*

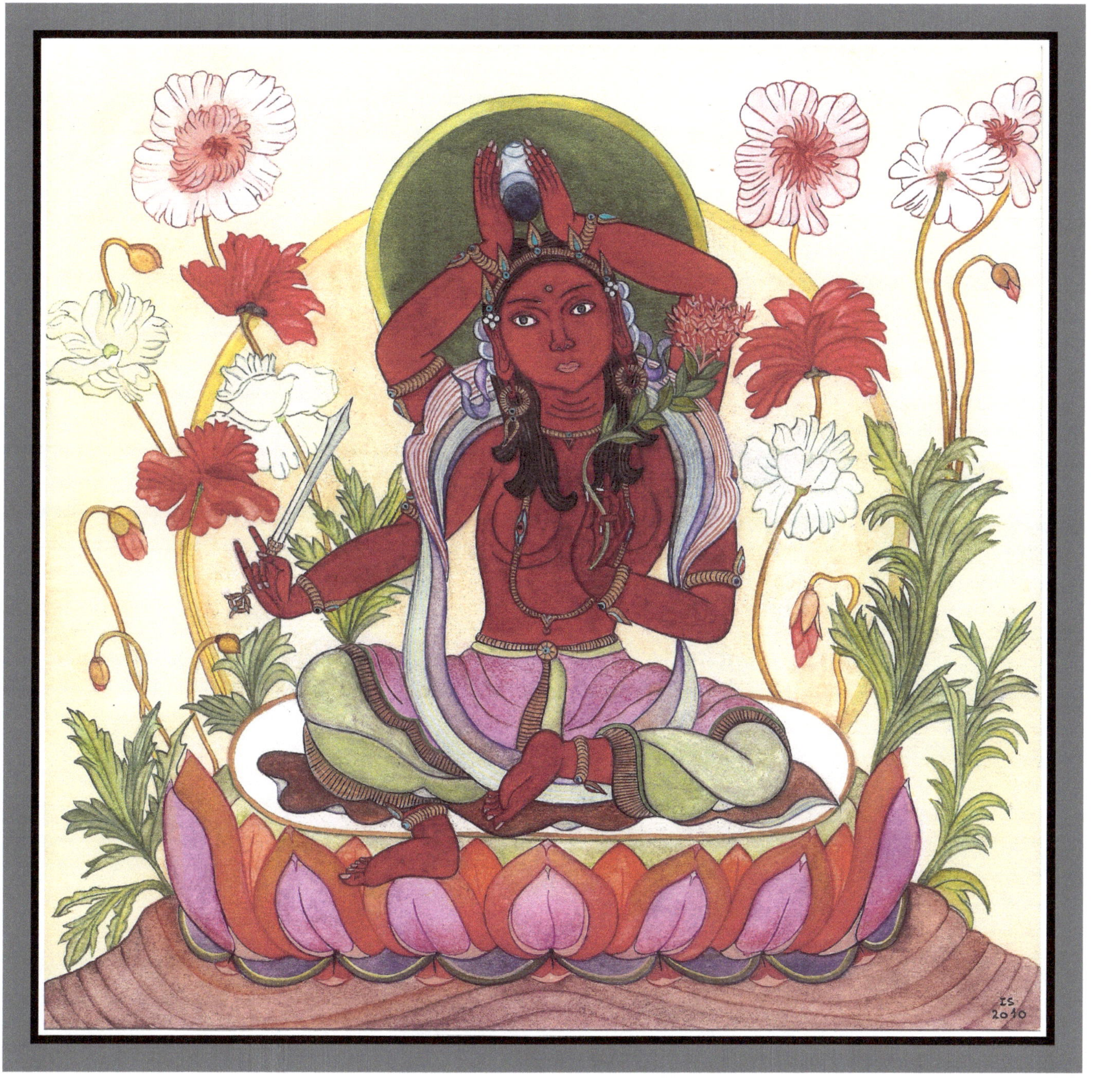
IS
2010

11. TĀRĀ SUMMONER OF ALL BEINGS, DISPELLER OF ALL MISFORTUNE
JAGAD-VAŚĪ VIPAN-NIRBARHAṆA-TĀRĀ

namaḥ samanta-bhū-pāla-
paṭalâkarṣana-kṣame
calad-bhṛkuṭī-hūṃ-kāra-
sarvâpada-vimocani

Homage! Her, Who can summon all
Earth-Protectors' great assemblies!
With HUM shouting, shaking, frowning,
Rescuing from all misfortune.

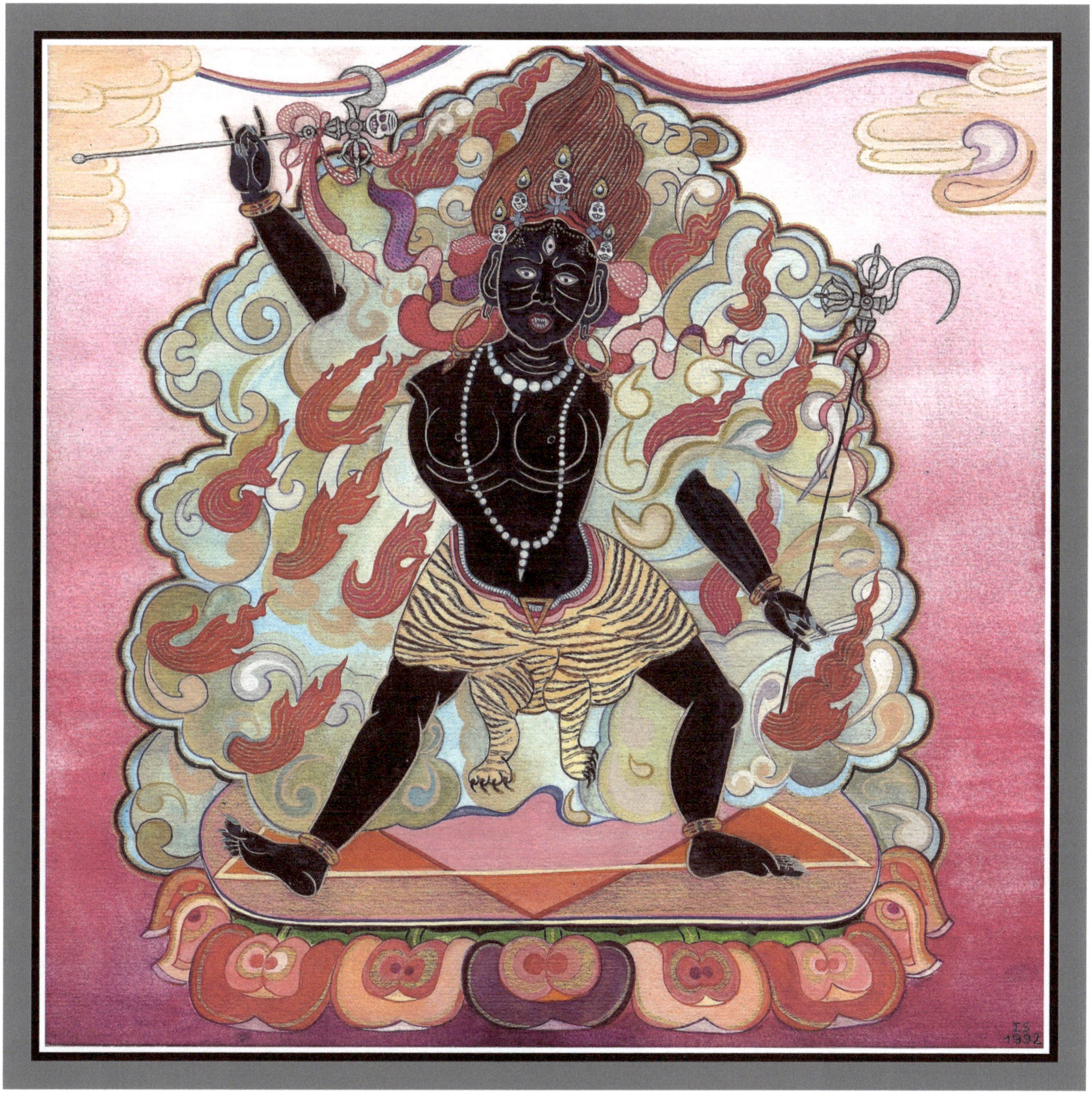
IS
1992

12. TĀRĀ GIVER OF ALL PROSPERITY
KALYĀNA-DA-TĀRĀ

namaḥ sikhaṇda-khaṇḍêndu-
mukuṭâbharanojjvale
amithāba-jatā-bhāra-
bhāsure kiraṇa-dhruve

Homage! Her mass of hair adorns
A diadem of crescent moon!
From Her hair-knot *Amitābha*
Emanates eternal light-rays.

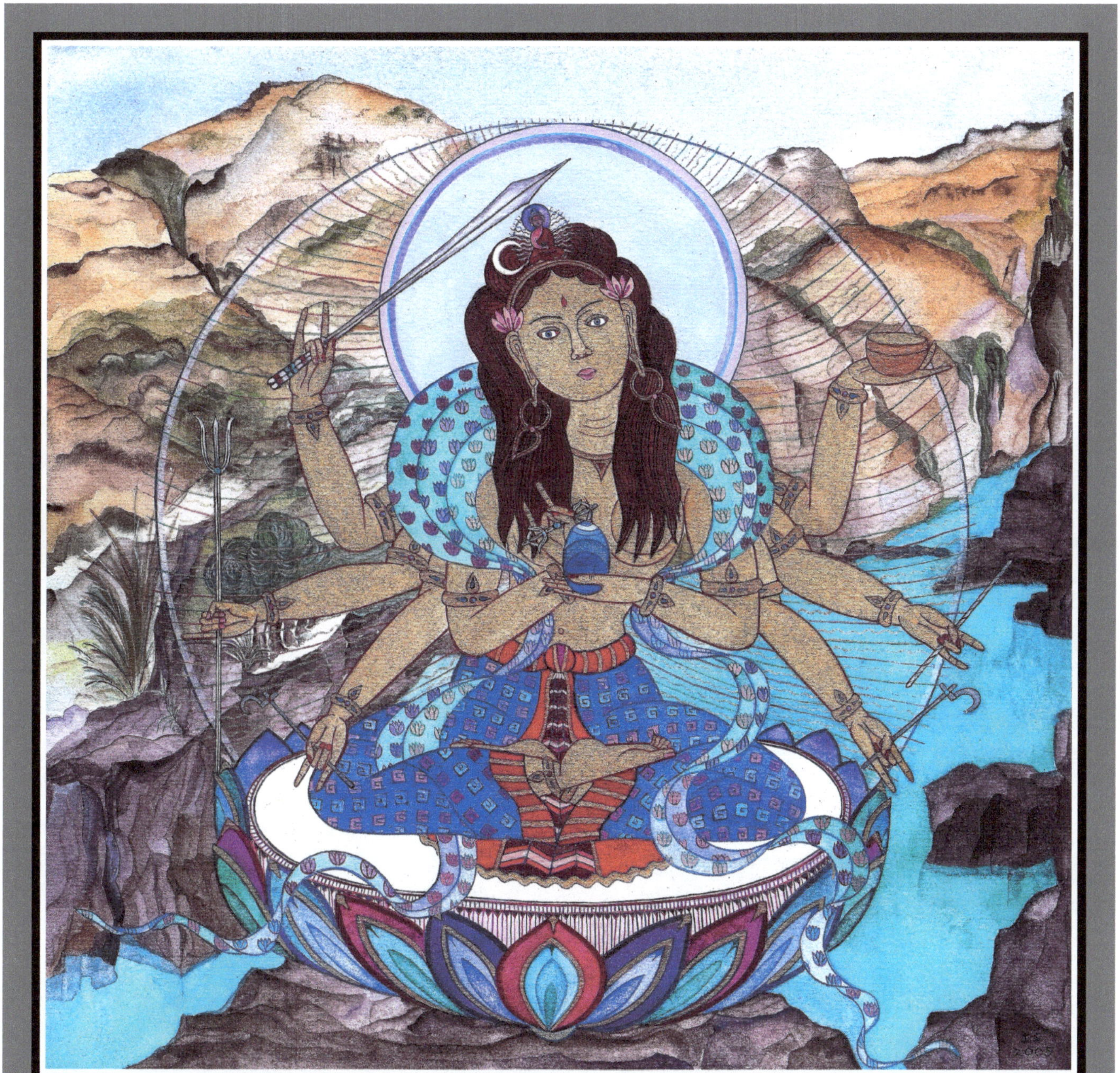

13. TĀRĀ THE RIPENER
PARIPĀCAKA-TĀRĀ

namaḥ kalpânta-hutabhug-
jvālā-mālântara-sthite
āliḍha-muditā-bandha-
ripu-cakra-vināśani

Homage! Who midst blazing garlands
Like eon-ending fires dwells!
Right leg outstretched, joyful ripening,
Subduing hosts of enemies.

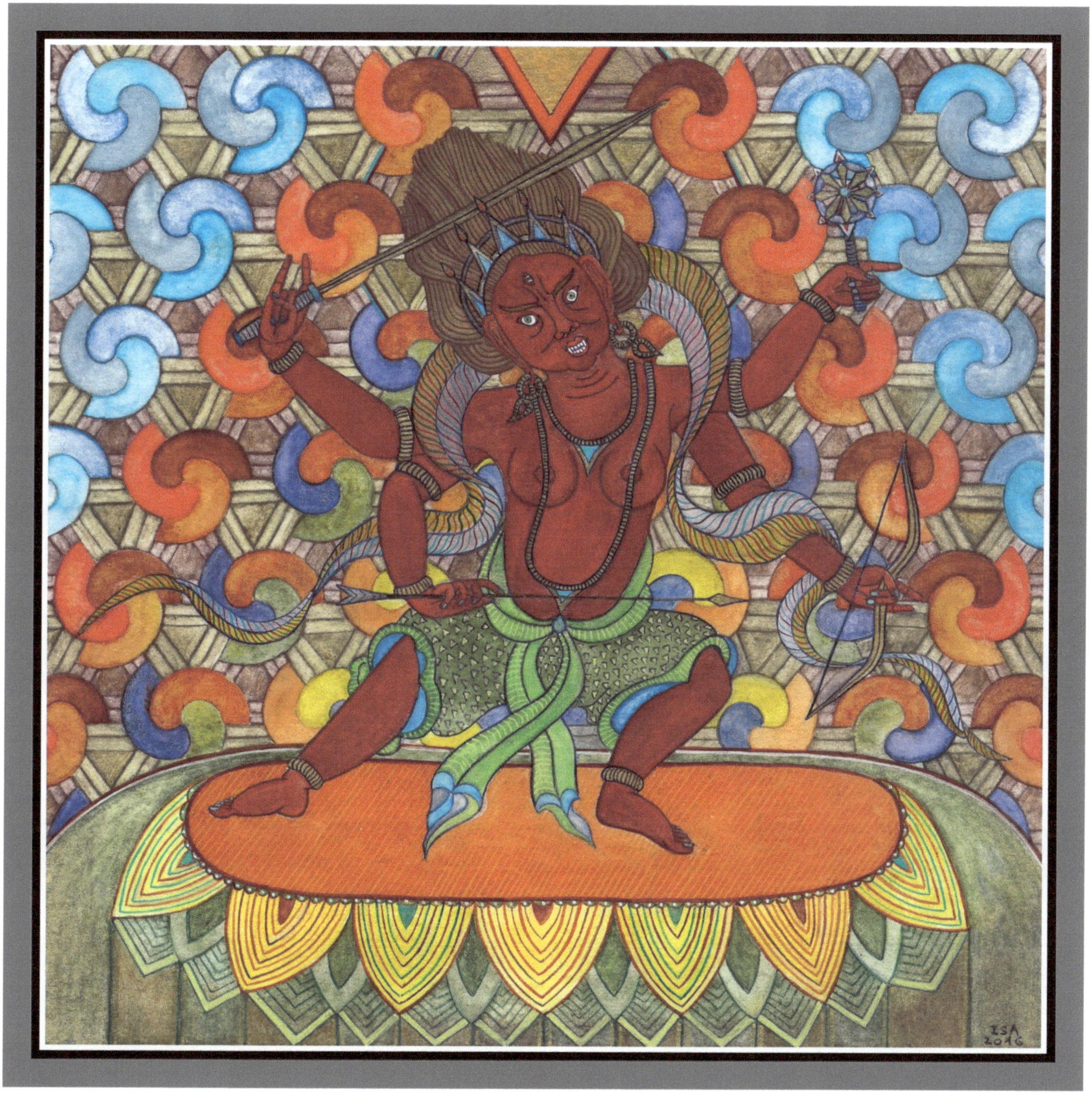
ISA
2016

14. TĀRĀ THE WRATHFUL SUMMONER
BHṚKUṬĪ-TĀRĀ

namaḥ kara-talâghāta-
caraṇâhata-bhū-tale
bhṛkuṭī-kṛta-hūṃ-kāra
sapta-pātāla-bhedini

Homage! Her, Whose palms the ground strike,
Whose heels are stamping on the earth!
With wrathful frowning uttering HUM
All Seven Underworlds are shattered.

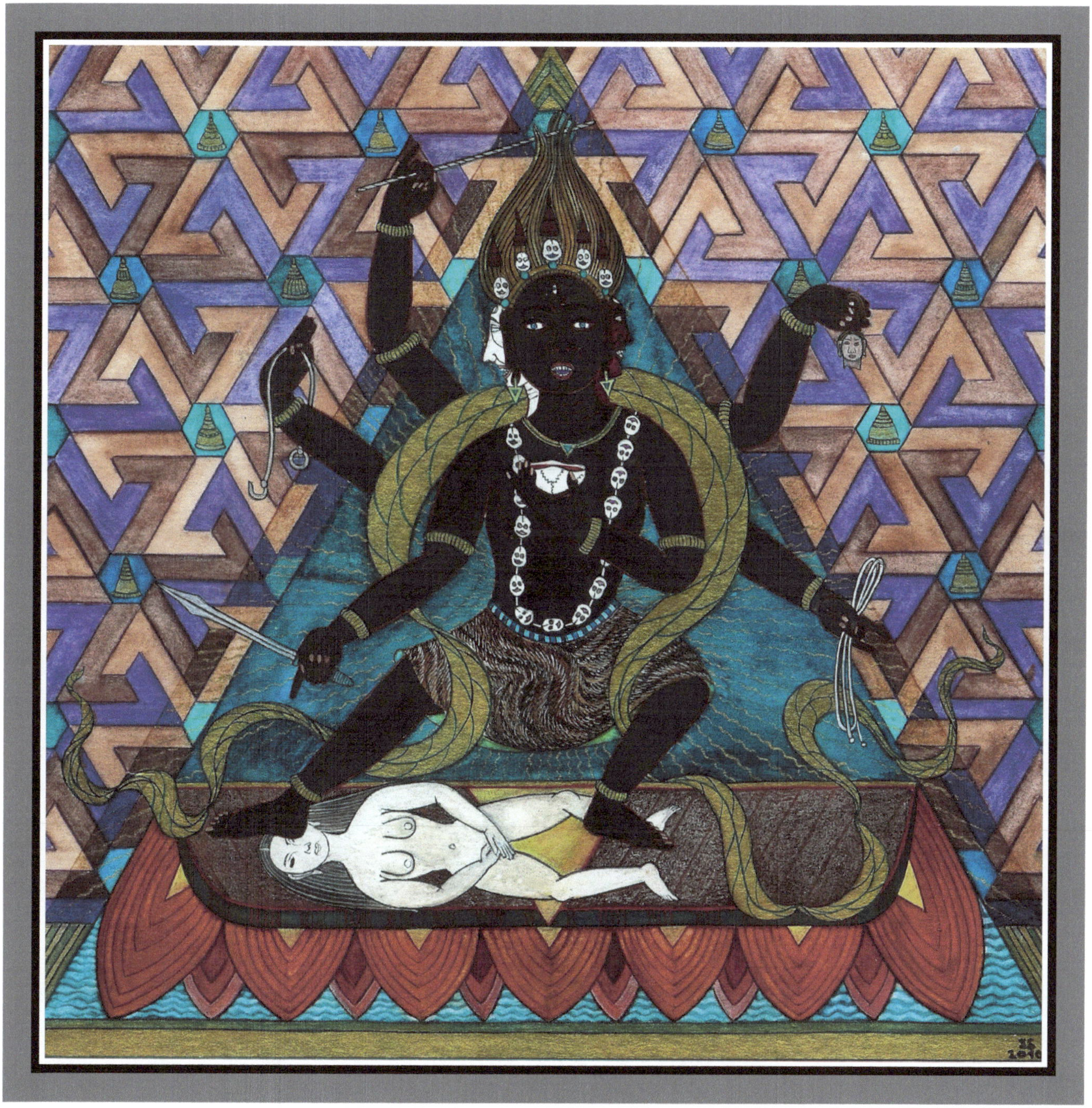
2010

15. TĀRĀ THE GREAT PEACEFUL ONE
MĀHA-ŚĀNTI-TĀRĀ

namaḥ sive subhe sānte
sānta nirvāna gocare
svāhā-pranava-saṃyukte
mahā-pātaka-nāśani

Homage! Peace, Nirvana Her field,
The happy virtuous, peaceful One!
Who, with chanting OM and SVAHA
All downfalls hinders and destroys.

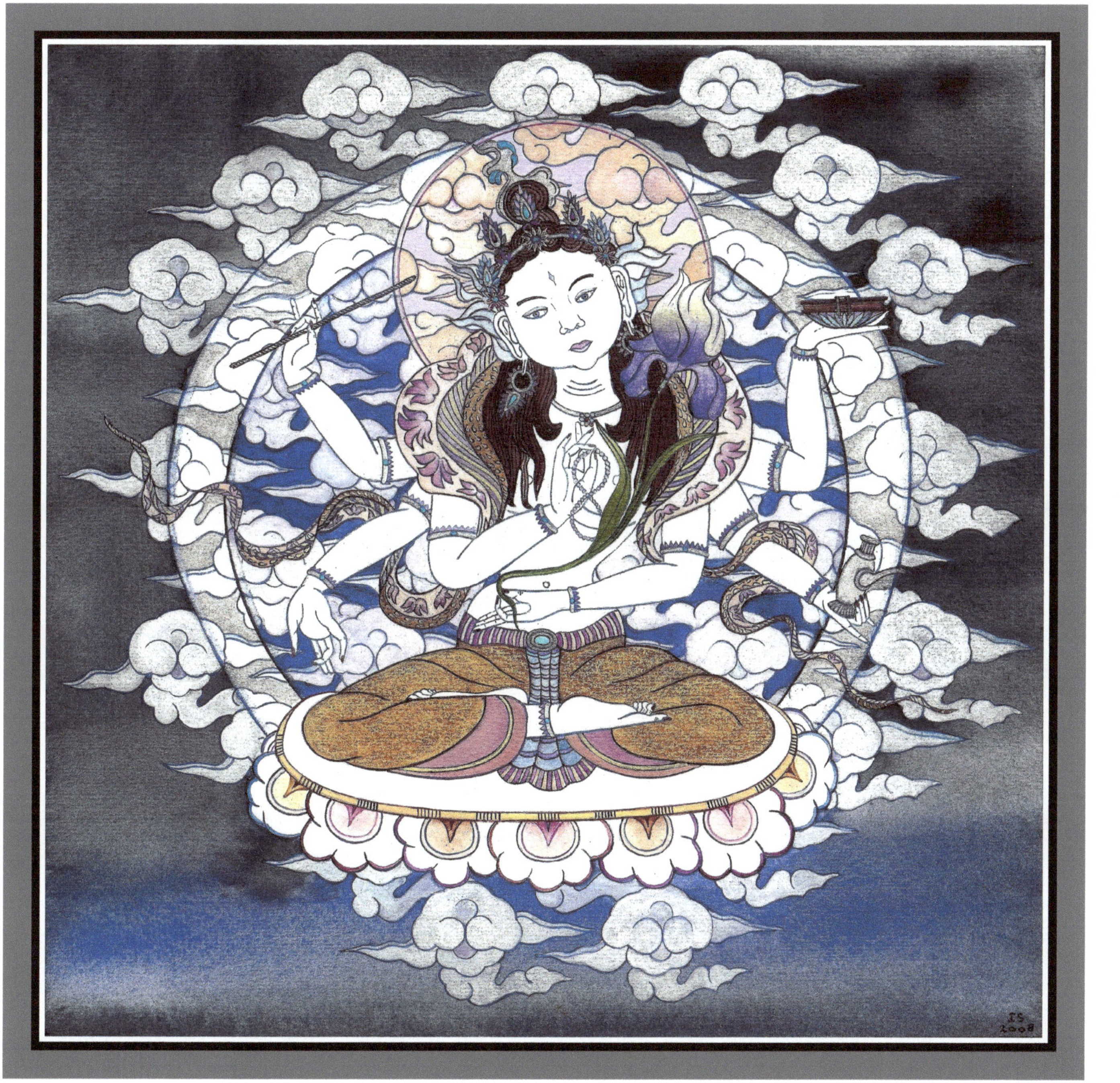

16. TĀRĀ DESTROYER OF ALL ATTACHEMENT
RĀGA-NIṢŪDANA-TĀRĀ

namaḥ pramuditâbandha-
ripu-gātra-prabhedini
daśâkṣara-pada-nyāse
vidya-hūṃ-kāra-dīpite

Homage! Who's surrounded by joy,
Subdues all the bodies of foes!
Ten syllables garland adorns
Rescuer through knowledge of HUM.

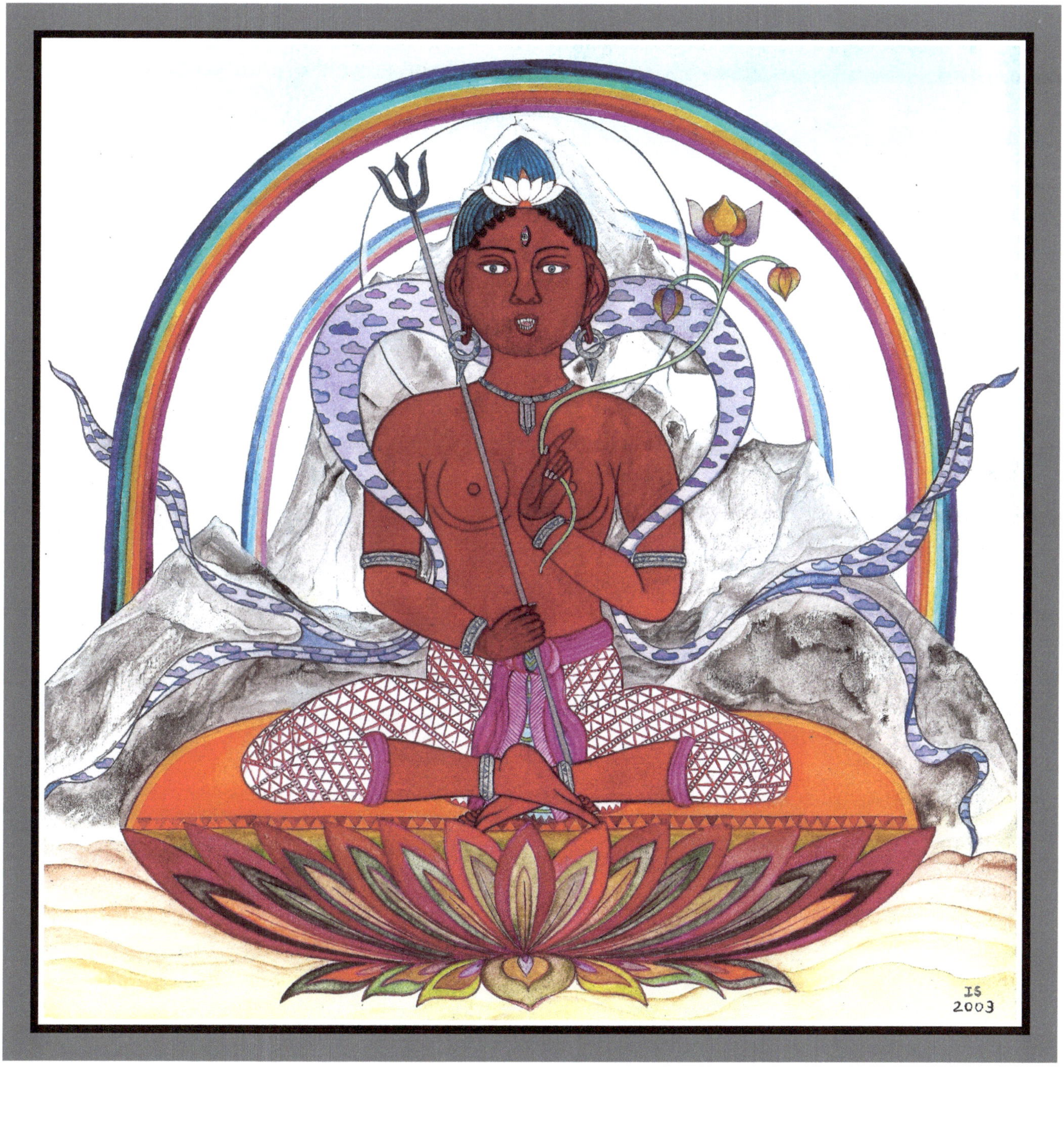
IS
2003

17. TĀRĀ ACCOMPLISHER OF ALL BLISS
SUKHA-SĀDHANA-TĀRĀ

namas ture padâghāta-
hūṃ-kārâkāra-bījite
meru-mandara-kailāsa-
bhuvana-traya-cālini

Homage! Her, Whose dancing stamping,
Born from seed with the shape of HUM!
The Three Worlds beneath Her tremble,
Mount *Kailāsh, Meru, Mandara*.

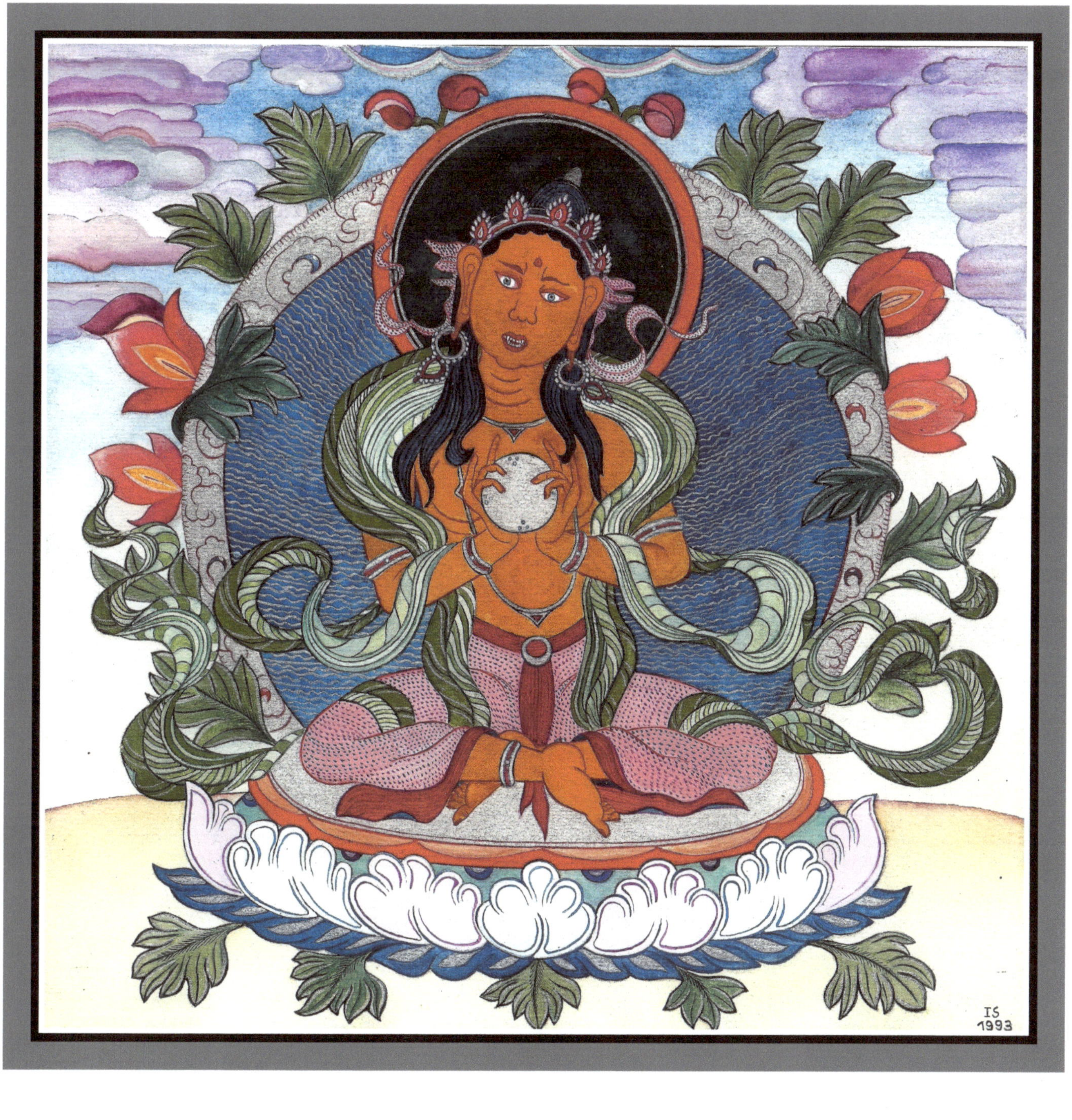
IS
1993

18. TĀRĀ THE VICTORIOUS
VIJAYA-TĀRĀ

namaḥ sura-sarâkāra-
hariṇânka-kara-sthite
tāra-dvir-ukta-phat-kāra
aśeṣa-viṣa-nāśani

Homage, Who holds the hare-marked moon,
Shining like the *Devas'* Clear Lake!
With chanting TARA twice and PHAT
All poisons are complete dispelled.

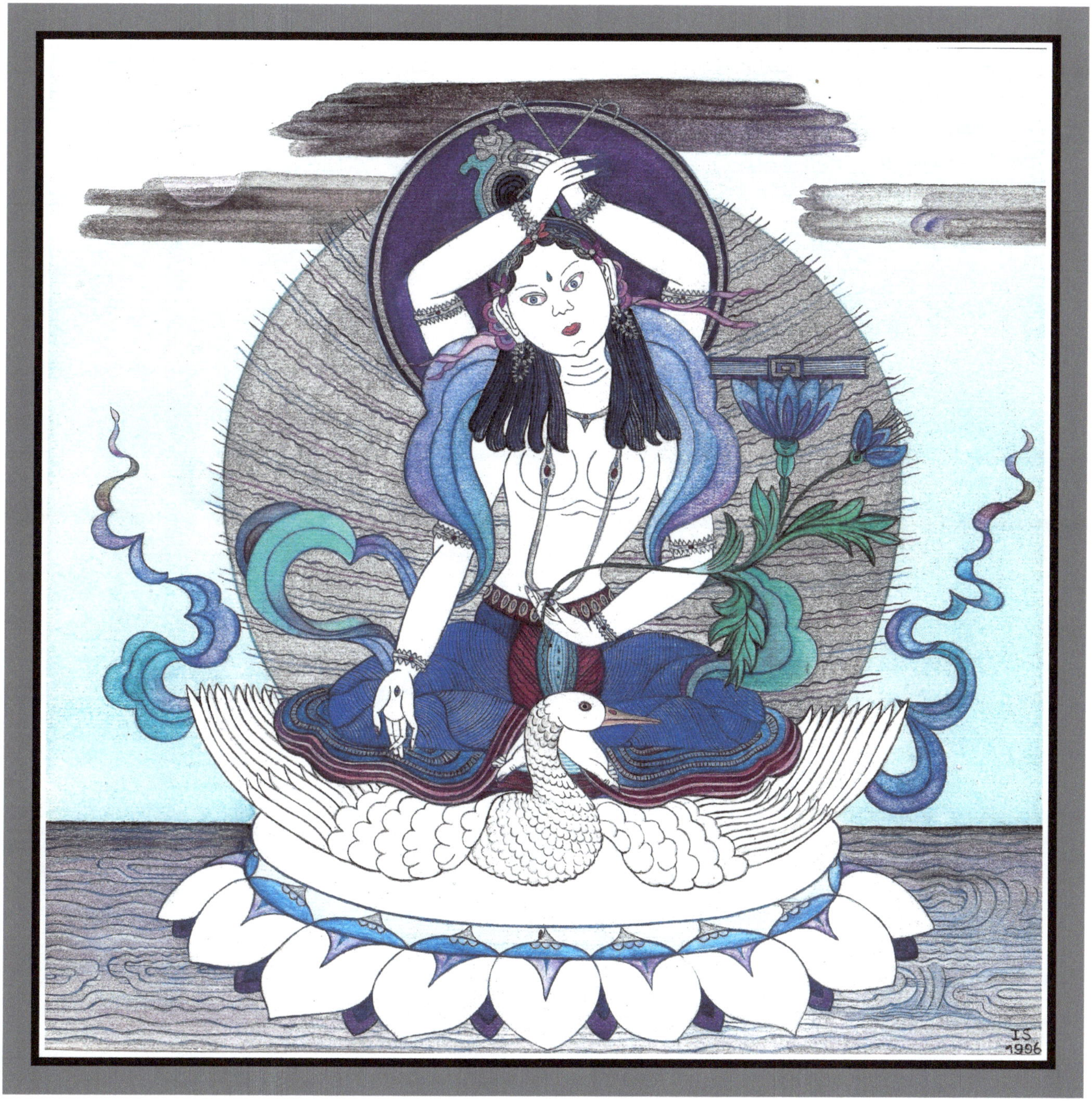
IS
1996

19. TĀRĀ CONSUMER OF ALL SUFFERING
DUḤKHA-DAHANA-TĀRĀ

namaḥ sura-gaṇâdyakṣa-
sura-kiṃnara-sevite
ābandha-muditâbhoga-
kali-duḥsvapna-nāśani

Homage! Her, Whom Three Worlds' rulers
Devas and *Kinnaras* honor!
Joy-producing shining armor
Dispelling bad dreams and conflict.

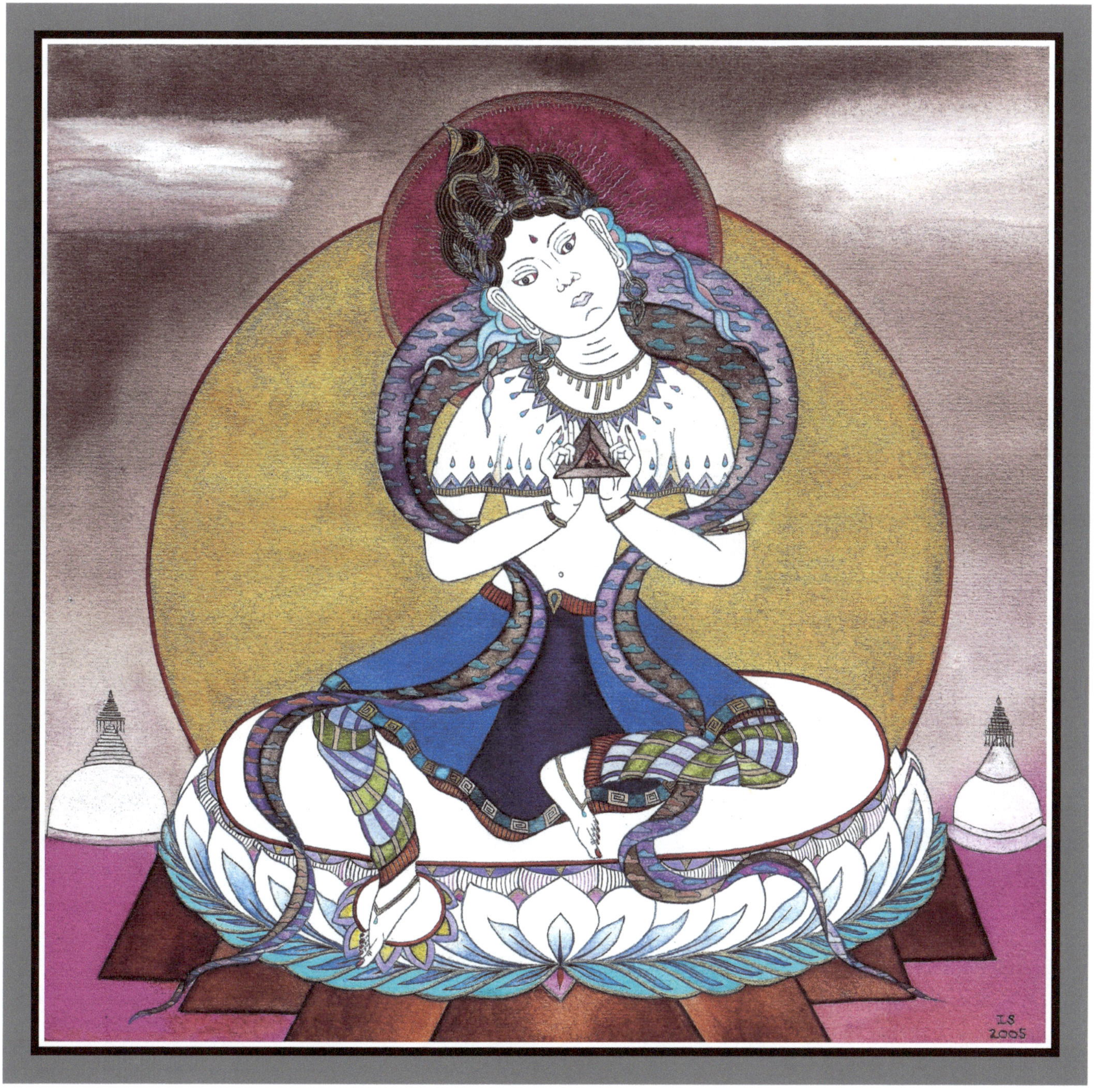
IS
2005

20. TĀRĀ SOURCE OF ALL ATTAINMENTS
SIDDHI-SAṂBHAVA-TĀRĀ

namaś-candrârka-sampurna-
nayana-dyuti-bhāsure
hara dvir-ukta-tuttāre
viṣama-jvara-nāśani

Homage! Her, Whose clear eyes are bright
With radiance of Sun and Moon!
With HARA twice and TUTTARE
Samsāras' fevers are dispelled.

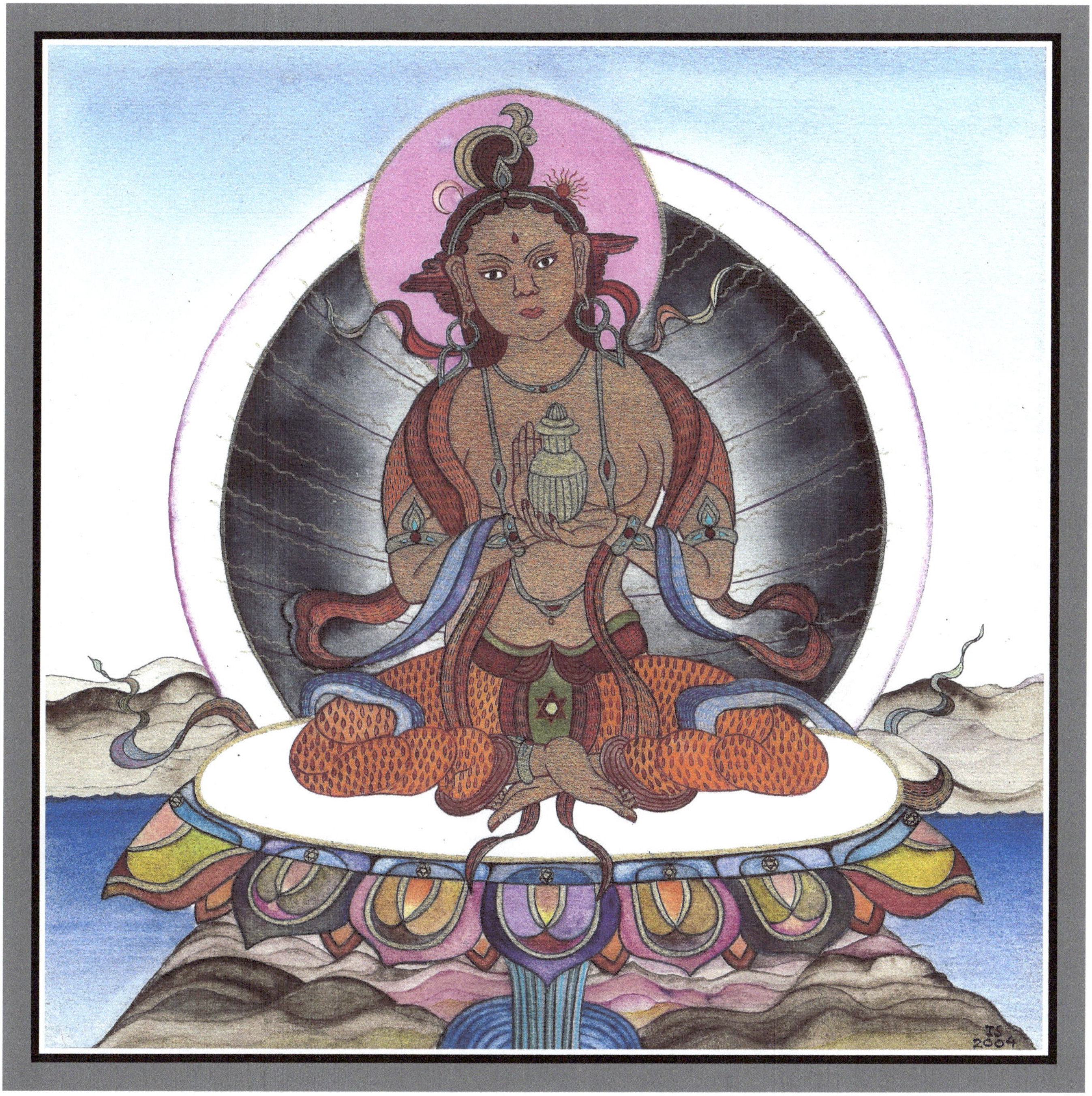
IS
2004

21. TĀRĀ THE PERFECTER
PARIPŪRAṆA-TĀRĀ

namas tri-tattva-vinyāsa-
śiva-śakti-samanvite
graha-vetala-yakṣâuga-
nāśani pravare ture

Homage! Her, Who's liberating
Within the Three Realities!
Crushing crowds of harmful forces
Supreme with TURE, Perfect One.

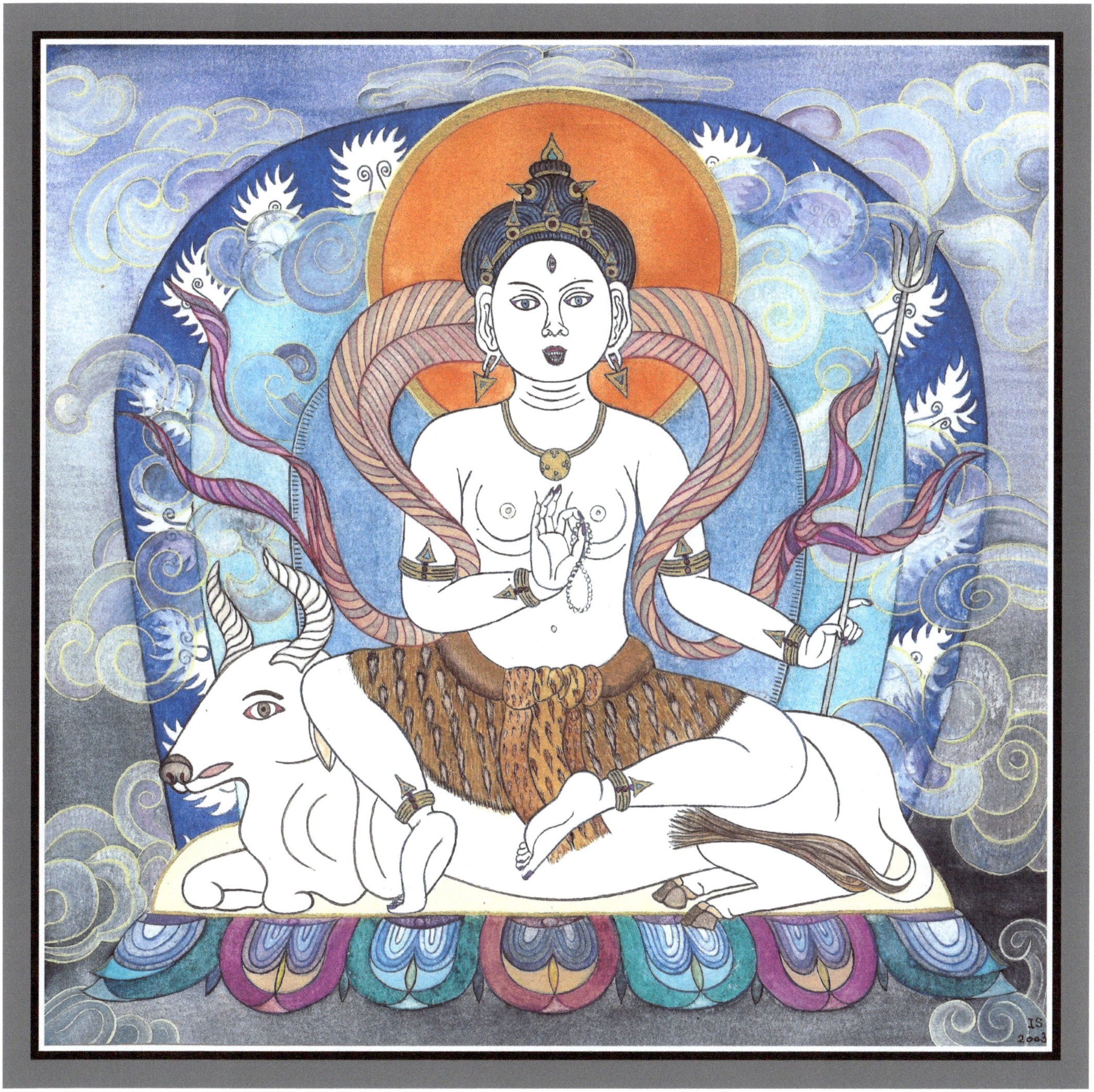
IS
2003

ABOUT THE ARTIST

SUSANNE ISABEL KRAJANEK

Born 1952 in Vienna, Austria

Technical education as engineer for industrial ceramics , building materials and glass at a technical college in Vienna.

More inclined to be an artist I continued my studies at the master class for Ceramics and Sculpture at the University of Applied Arts in Vienna.

Living and travelling on the pilgrimage routes of northern India and Nepal with my family ever since 1976 when I arrived in India for the first time with my husband and baby daughter, this places have become the 'native realm' and content of my art.

Since many years the Old Burmese Monastery in Bodhgaya in Bihar, north central India, has become the main place for me to stay, alternated with long pilgrimages in the mountains of Gharwal and travels to Burma and Vietnam.

Mostly the rivers, mountains and temples of Northern India give me the ideas for my paintings,

Other publications :

DON'T MAKE A SIGN ON THE BOAT, STORIES FROM BURMA

Paintings: isabelkrajanek.deviantart.com

www.ingramcontent.com/pod-product-compliance
Lightning Source LLC
Chambersburg PA
CBHW050810180526
45159CB00004B/1622
* 9 7 8 1 5 4 1 0 8 7 5 0 7 *